# Table of Contents

A. INTRODUCTION .................................................. 1
   1. Recent legislation involving sex offenses against children ................ 1
   2. Typology and number of offenses ................................. 1
   3. Table of statutes, guidelines, and sentences ......................... 2
   4. Methodology ................................................. 3

B. PORNOGRAPHY ................................................... 5
   1. Statutory provisions ........................................... 5
   2. Indexing and cross references among statutes and guidelines ........... 5
   3. Production Guideline 2G2.1 ..................................... 6
   4. Trafficking/Receipt Guideline 2G2.2 .............................. 9
   5. Possession Guideline 2G2.4 ..................................... 12
   6. The use of substantial assistance motions in child pornography sentencing .......... 13

C. TRANSPORTATION ................................................. 14
   1. Statutory provisions ........................................... 14
   2. Transportation Guideline 2G1.2 .................................. 15

D. CRIMINAL SEXUAL ABUSE ......................................... 16
   1. Statutory provisions ........................................... 16
   2. Analysis of sentences imposed under Aggravated Sexual Abuse Guideline 2A3.1 .... 18
   3. Sexual Abuse of a Minor Guideline 2A3.2 .......................... 21
   4. Analysis of sentences imposed under Abusive Sexual Contact Guideline 2A3.4 ...... 24

E. THE USE OF COMPUTERS IN CHILD PORNOGRAPHY DISTRIBUTION ......... 25
   1. Ways that computers can be used to disseminate pornography ........... 25
   2. Public and congressional concerns about pornography and computers ..... 27
   3. Cyberporn and culpability ...................................... 28
   4. Computer use among federal pornography defendants ................. 29
   5. Punishing the use of computers to spread child pornography ........... 30

F. TARGETING DANGEROUS OFFENDERS ................................ 31
   1. The dangers of sex offenses against children ....................... 31
   2. Current guidelines take multiple approaches to targeting dangerous offenders ....... 33
   3. Risk classification of child sexual abusers ......................... 34
   4. Implications for sentencing policy ................................ 36

G. RECOMMENDATIONS .............................................. 37
   1. Guideline amendments submitted to Congress in 1996 ................. 37
   2. Recommendation for increased statutory maximum penalties ............ 38
   3. Amendments currently under consideration by the Commission .......... 39

A.  **INTRODUCTION**

1.  **Recent legislation involving sex offenses against children**

The Sex Crimes Against Children Prevention Act of 1995 (SCACPA), Pub. L. No. 104-71, 109 Stat. 774, directed the Sentencing Commission to increase sentencing guideline offense levels for crimes involving child pornography, prostitution, and other offenses, and to add penalty enhancements for use of a computer in child pornography cases. Guideline amendments to increase these penalties were sent to Congress for review on April 30, 1996. They will become effective on November 1, 1996, barring further action by Congress.

In addition, the Telecommunications Act of 1996 created a new offense involving the persuasion, inducement, enticement or coercion of a minor, in areas under federal jurisdiction or by means of interstate or foreign commerce, to engage in prostitution or other prohibited sexual activity. Amendments to incorporate this new offense into the guidelines were also sent to Congress for review.

Section 6 of the SCACPA directed the Commission to prepare a report concerning offenses involving child pornography and other sex offenses against children. It is, of course, too early to evaluate the effectiveness of the increased punishment that will result from the recent legislation. We can, however, study sentencing under the statutes and guidelines that are currently in effect.

2.  **Typology and number of offenses**

Federal sex offenses against children can be divided into three groups — pornography, transportation, and criminal sexual abuse. The sentencing guidelines and this report are similarly divided. The **pornography** guidelines involve convictions under 18 U.S.C. §§ 2251 and 2252. Guideline 2G2.1 covers offenses involving the **production** of pornography, such as taking sexually explicit photographs of minors or advertising for minors to participate in such production. Guideline 2G2.2 covers **trafficking** in child pornography, such as maintaining a computer bulletin board from which subscribers can "download" child pornography, or sending pornographic material through the mail. **Receipt** of such material is also covered under §2G2.2. Guideline 2G2.4 involves **possession** of three or more items of child pornography.

The **transportation** guideline, 2G1.2, covers convictions under 8 U.S.C. § 1329 and 18 U.S.C. §§ 2421, 2422 and 2423(a). The statute covers transportation of a minor for purposes of either **prostitution** or **other prohibited sexual conduct**. In practice, most cases that do not involve prostitution involve sexual abuse. **Criminal sexual abuse** in its various degrees of seriousness is prosecuted under 18 U.S.C. §§ 2241-2244. The most serious is **aggravated sexual abuse**, which includes rape by means of force, threats, or coercion, and any sexual acts with a child under the age of 12. **Abusive sexual contact** involves forcible or coercive touching of the sexual areas without a sexual act involving penetration. **Sexual abuse of a minor** involves non-forcible sex with a person between the ages of 12 and 16 with at least a four year age difference.

Sex crimes against children represent a small proportion of all federal criminal sentencings. During 1995, 58 defendants were sentenced for child pornography offenses, representing 0.2% of the total number of federal sentencings that year.[1] Six defendants were sentenced for transportation of a minor, representing 0.02% of all federal sentencings. In the same year, 145 defendants were sentenced for some form of criminal sexual abuse of a victim under 18 years of age,[2] representing 0.4% of all federal sentencings in 1995.

Federal sexual abuse convictions also represent a small proportion of the total number of nationwide convictions for sexual abuse of minors. Using the most recently published data, it is estimated that in one year there were approximately 8,662 convictions for the rape of a minor in state courts.[3] Based on this estimate, federal convictions would account for approximately 1.6% of such convictions nationwide. Because data are not available, similar comparisons cannot be undertaken regarding pornography offenses.

### 3. Table of statutes, guidelines, and sentences

As a quick reference, Table 1 on page 4 displays the statutes punishing sex offenses against children and the corresponding sentencing guidelines that are discussed in this report. Offenders convicted under a particular statute may be sentenced under another guideline through

---

[1] The total number of cases sentenced during fiscal year 1995 was 38,500. UNITED STATES SENTENCING COMMISSION ANNUAL REPORT 1995 36, Table 8.

[2] The criteria for inclusion of these cases was (1) they were sentenced during fiscal year 1995, (2) they included a conviction under 18 U.S.C. §§ 2241-2244, and (3) the victim was less than 18 years old.

[3] State court data on the number of sexual abuse cases involving a minor victim is not available at the national level. An estimate was derived on the number of these cases using information on state court convictions and offense characteristics of state prison inmates, as reported in two recent publications by the Bureau of Justice Statistics (BJS). These two publications represent the most current information available on all state court actions and state prison populations. The BJS reported 21,655 rape convictions in state courts during 1992. BUREAU OF JUSTICE STATISTICS, U.S. DEP'T OF JUSTICE, SOURCEBOOK 1994, Table 5.46 (1995). BJS recently published a monograph on crimes involving child victims. BUREAU OF JUSTICE STATISTICS, U.S. DEP'T OF JUSTICE, CHILD VICTIMIZERS: VIOLENT OFFENDERS AND THEIR VICTIMS (March, 1996). This report, based upon a survey of inmates in state prisons conducted during 1991, found that approximately 40 percent of prison inmates incarcerated for forcible rape committed their crimes against a victim less than 18 years of age. *Id.* at 1. Applying this proportion (40%) to the number of state convictions for rape (21,655) yields an estimate of 8,662 state rapes involving victims under 18 years of age. The 145 federal cases in 1995 include a broad range of sexual behavior, including sexual contact, statutory rape and rape. State convictions for forcible rape likely do not include the less severe offense conduct used in the federal analysis. As a result, 8,662 may under-represent the total number of state court convictions for offenses similar to the 145 federal cases analyzed.

the operation of cross references contained in the *Guidelines Manual*. These cross references are listed, as are the number of cases sentenced under each guideline from 1994 through 1995, the current base offense levels (BOLs), the BOLs as amended in the proposals sent to Congress this year, the sentencing guideline ranges corresponding to each year, and the average sentences that have been imposed for each offense. The BOL is the basic sentence range without any adjustments or aggravating factors such as criminal history, age of the victim, etc. As reflected in the average sentence column, most offenders receive sentences longer than the BOL based on these aggravating factors. More detailed descriptions of the statutory provisions covered by these guidelines are provided in later sections of this report.

**4.     Methodology**

All 1994 and 1995 cases with convictions for the above referenced statutes were analyzed for this study – a total of 469 cases. Of these, 423 met the statutory criteria and involved victims of less than 18 years of age. Information already collected as part of the regular Commission Monitoring Database was supplemented by collecting additional information relevant to the proposed amendments. Information was gathered concerning:

- the nature of the offense conduct (*e.g.* the extent of pornography trafficking activity)
- whether a computer was used in the offense, and if so, how
- the impact of any plea agreement on the sentence
- the location of the sentence within the guideline range
- the type of assistance offered by defendants receiving a substantial assistance departure
- the criminal history of the offender, especially regarding sex offenses
- information regarding any pattern of sexual abuse or sexual exploitation of children
- information concerning any substance abuse or mental disorder of the defendant
- whether the offense conduct involved prostitution or other prohibited conduct
- the number of victims involved, their ages, and their relationship to the defendant

Each particular sentencing guideline raises different issues, as discussed in Sections devoted to each guideline below. Section E analyzes the use of computers in sexual offenses against children. Section F discusses the use of criminal history and other factors used in identifying repeat sex offenders. Section G contains recommendations for amendment of current statutes and guidelines.

## Table 1: Statutes and Guidelines Concerning Sex Offenses Against Children

| Statutes | Guideline | Cross Reference(s) | Number of Analyzed Cases*** | Current BOL (Sentence Range in Months)* | Proposed BOL (Sentence Range in Months)** | Current Average Sentence (Months) |
|---|---|---|---|---|---|---|
| 18 U.S.C. §§ 2241; 2242; 2423(b) | 2A3.1 criminal sexual abuse | 2A1.1 | 130 | 27 (70-87) | No change | 130 |
| 18 U.S.C. §§ 2243(a); 2423(b) | 2A3.2 criminal sexual abuse of a minor (statutory rape) | 2A3.1 | 52 | 15 (18-24) | No change | 21 |
| 18 U.S.C. § 2244(a)(1),(2),(3) | 2A3.4 abusive sexual contact | 2A3.1; 2A3.2 | 103 | 10-16 (6-27) | No change | 22 |
| 8 U.S.C. § 1328; 18 U.S.C. §§ 2421; 2422(b); 2423(a) | 2G1.2 transportation of a minor for purposes of prostitution or prohibited sexual conduct | 2A3.1; 2A3.2; 2A3.4; 2G2.1 | 10 | 16 (21-27) | | 44 |
| 18 U.S.C. § 2251 (a),(b),(c)(1)(B) | 2G2.1 sexual exploitation of a minor by production of material | | 22 | 25 (57-71) | 27+2 for computer use (70-87) | 79 |
| 18 U.S.C. §§ 2251(c)(1)(A); 2252(a)(1),(2),(3) | 2G2.2 trafficking in child pornography | 2A3.1; 2A3.2; 2A3.4; 2G2.1 | 66 | 15 (18-24) | 17+2 for computer use (24-30) | 29 |
| 18 U.S.C. § 2252(a)(4) | 2G2.4 possession of child pornography | 2G2.1; 2G2.2 | 24 | 13 (12-18) | 15+2 for computer use (18-24) | 15 |

\* The sentencing range listed would apply only to first-time offenders and does not reflect any of the adjustments that may result in a higher or lower sentence.

\*\* The sentencing range listed would apply only to first-time offenders and does not reflect either the adjustments that may result in a higher or lower sentence or the two-level increase listed for computer use.

\*\*\* Sixteen additional cases convicted under the pornography statutes were cross-referenced to the sexual abuse guidelines. These cases were not included in the analysis of the sexual abuse guidelines because Congress requested an analysis of cases by statute of conviction.

## B. PORNOGRAPHY

### 1. Statutory provisions

As shown in Table 1, several statutory provisions relate to the sexual exploitation of a minor through the production, trafficking, and possession of pornography. These are sentenced under guidelines in Chapter Two, Part G, Sections 2.1- 2.5. This report is limited to those provisions that are the subject of directives in the SCACPA. Offenses under 18 U.S.C. § 2251 generally cover conduct relating to the production of visual depictions involving minors engaged in sexually explicit conduct. The penalty for a violation of § 2251 is imprisonment of not more than 10 years, a fine, or both. The penalty for a violation of § 2251 if the defendant has a prior conviction under chapters 109A or 110 of such title is a fine, imprisonment of between five and 15 years, or both.

Subsections (a) and (b) of 18 U.S.C. § 2251 apply when the offense directly involves minors in the production of pornography. Subsections (c)(1)(A) and (B) apply to publishing notices or advertisements either to traffic in child pornography or to participate in its production. Sections 2252(a)(1), (2) and (3) cover trafficking or receipt of child pornography. The penalty for these offenses is imprisonment of not more than 10 years, a fine, or both. If the defendant has a prior conviction under chapters 109A or 110, the sentence is imprisonment of between five and 15 years. The final section, § 2252(a)(4), concerns possession of child pornography. The statutory penalties for this section are imprisonment of not more than five years, a fine, or both.

### 2. Indexing and cross references among statutes and guidelines

Child pornography offenses covered by this study are sentenced under three guidelines. Guideline 2G2.1 concerns the production of child pornography, §2G2.2 concerns trafficking and receipt, and §2G2.4 concerns possession. The production guideline generally entails the most severe punishment, with a base offense level of 25. The trafficking/receipt guideline has a base offense level of 15, and the possession guideline has a base offense level of 13.

The statutory index in the *Guidelines Manual* assigns cases to the guideline that is deemed most appropriate, given the conduct charged in the count(s) of conviction. However, because offenders sometimes are convicted under statutes that do not accurately describe their actual offense conduct, many guidelines have cross references to guidelines with higher offense levels. This ensures that the guideline sentence will more appropriately fit the seriousness of the actual criminal conduct. For example, the trafficking/receipt guideline has a cross reference to the production guideline "[i]f the offense conduct involved causing . . . a minor to engage in sexually explicit conduct for the purpose of producing a visual depiction of such conduct," and if the resulting offense level is greater than it would be under the trafficking/receipt guideline.

### 3. Production Guideline 2G2.1

#### a. Analysis of Sentences Imposed

This guideline has a base offense level of 25, a four-level enhancement if the offense involved a minor under 12 and a two-level enhancement if the minor was 12 or older but had not attained the age of 16. It also includes a two-level enhancement if the defendant was a parent, relative, or legal guardian of the minor or if the minor was in the custody, care, or supervisory control of the defendant. A special instruction is included to increase punishment for multiple victims.

Thus, if the defendant used a minor under 12 in the production of sexually explicit material, the offense level would be 29. A first time offender would face a sentence of imprisonment of between 87 and 108 months. If more than one minor under 12 was exploited, the defendant's guideline range would be 108-135 months. If the court granted a three-level downward adjustment for acceptance of responsibility, the guideline range would be 63-78 months and 78-97 months, respectively.

During 1994 and 1995, a total of 22 defendants were sentenced under this guideline. About two-thirds of the defendants (n=14) were so sentenced because they were charged and convicted of offenses referenced directly to this guideline. The remaining third were convicted of less serious charges but were nevertheless cross-referenced to the pornography production guideline from either §2G1.2 (n=2), §2G2.2 (n=2), or §2G2.4 (n=4). The average prison sentence for these cases was 79.2 months. Eighty-one percent were sentenced within the guideline range. These 17 cases were distributed uniformly across the entire range. Nineteen percent (n=4) received either a substantial assistance departure (n=2) or other downward departure (n=2). No cases received an upward departure.

The amount of prison time that is appropriate for these offenses is a policy judgment to be made by Congress and the Sentencing Commission. This judgment can be informed, however, by data on how the range of punishments available under the present guidelines are being used. Increasing offense levels far above that which is believed to be appropriate by practitioners in the courts could lead to improper charges or departures intended to result in lower sentences. [4]

A review of the legislative history of 18 U.S.C. § 2251, beginning with its enactment in the Protection of Children Against Sexual Exploitation Act of 1977, reveals that Congress intended to criminalize the use of foreign or interstate commerce [5] for the production of child

---

[4] For a review of such problems with other federal penalty statutes, see Stephen J. Schulhofer, *Rethinking Mandatory Minimums*, 28 WAKE FOREST L. REV. 199 (1993).

[5] In the report accompanying the Protection of Children Against Sexual Exploitation Act of 1977, the Senate Judiciary Committee stated, "[t]he committee is aware that Section 2251 may literally encompass isolated, individual acts involving the use of children in the production of

pornography, whether or not (1) the scale of the operation was large-scale or small-scale,[6] or (2) involved a commercial purpose.[7]

In about half of the cases, production involved engaging in a sexual act with one or several victims. However, these production cases generally do not reach the scale of commercial pornography. The production guideline makes no distinction between production for commercial purposes and production for personal, non-commercial use. Only a minority of cases sentenced under this guideline involve the production of pornography for commercial distribution. The following is the most extreme example we reviewed of a defendant attempting professional publication.

> *Case 212899. Defendant met young boys through the Big Brother organization and through trips to Mexico and Thailand. Numerous photographs were taken and developed by the defendant of at least 14 boys, appearing to be between the ages of 10 to 18. The photos depicted the boys posing nude, engaged in masturbation, or in mutual masturbation or oral sex with the defendant. Defendant also possessed commercially made child pornography from the 1960s, 1970s and early 1980s. Two letters dated from the early 1980s, one from a pornography publisher in Sweden and the other in Denmark, indicate that the defendant had tried to get some of his photographs published in these countries. However, the photographs were rejected. Defendant had no criminal history. Offense level was 30 (BOL 25, + 4 for victim under 12, + 4 for multiple counts, - 3 for acceptance of responsibility). Defendant was sentenced near top of the 97- 121 month guideline range, 120 months.*

Some defendants are sentenced under the production guideline by means of a cross reference, although they are convicted of receiving or possessing child pornography. For example, searches of the home of persons arrested after receiving a controlled delivery of pornographic materials may uncover photographs taken by the defendant for his own use. In such cases, the defendant's act of taking the photograph can be sufficient for the application of the production guideline.

> *Case 193448. Records from a mail-order pornography operation indicated the defendant had ordered 22 pornographic items involving juveniles. Defendant was*

---

sexually explicit materials. Section 2251 is not intended to reach all such isolated incidents, which often are more appropriately the subject of state or local concern. The Committee fully intends that federal prosecutors will wisely exercise their discretion to reach only those cases which are the proper subject of Federal concern."

[6]*See* S. Rep. No. 438, 95th Cong., 1st Sess. (1977), reprinted in 1978 U.S.C.C.A.N. 40, 47.

[7]*See* H.R.. Rep. No. 536, 98th Cong., 1st Sess. (1984), reprinted in 1984 U.S.C.C.A.N. 492, 493.

*sent a solicitation from a Postal Inspection Service undercover operation, from which he then ordered a video tape and a magazine containing explicit sexual contact between minors, some of which were under age 12. After a controlled delivery, a search of the defendant's home uncovered these materials as well as five Polaroid photographs of a partially clothed 15-year-old male. Although the defendant was convicted of receiving child pornography, the court sentenced him under the production guideline. Offense level was 24 (BOL 25, + 2 for victim under 16 at time photos taken, - 3 for acceptance or responsibility). Two previous convictions for minor theft resulted in a criminal history Category I. Defendant was sentenced at the bottom of the guideline range, 51 months.*

### b. Amendments submitted to Congress in 1996

In response to the Congressional directives contained in the SCACPA, the Commission adopted and submitted guideline amendments to Congress on April 30, 1996.[8] With respect to the production guideline, the Commission increased the base offense level in §2G2.1 by two levels for offenses under 18 U.S.C. § 2251. Based on Commission data discussed above about the use of the range of punishments available under the present guidelines, the Commission does not recommend an increase of more than two levels at this time.

The Commission also performed a prison impact analysis to discover how many "person-years" of prison resources will be required by the two-level BOL increase forwarded to Congress on April 30, 1996. Person-years is a standardized measure of the prison resources required to sentence one year's cases under a particular guideline. This increase will require the Bureau of Prisons to house the 13 people sentenced under the guideline in a typical recent year for about 16 months longer than under current practice.

In addition to implementing the directives contained in the SCACPA, the Commission added a two level enhancement in §2G2.1 if a computer was used to solicit participation in sexually explicit conduct by or with a minor for the purposes of producing a visual depiction of that conduct, in violation of 18 U.S.C. § 2251(c)(1)(B). Finally, the Commission recommends that Congress raise the statutory maximum penalties for child pornography production offenses under § 2251 from ten years to fifteen years for the reasons discussed below in Section G.

### 4. Trafficking/Receipt Guideline 2G2.2

#### a. Analysis of sentences imposed

The trafficking/receipt guideline takes a different approach to apportioning punishment than does the production guideline just discussed. Although it has a base offense level of 15 (in contrast to the production base offense level of 25), there are a number of very significant

---

[8] Amendments to the Sentencing Guidelines for United States Courts, 61 Fed. Reg. 20,306 (1996).

adjustments that can more than double the offense level, resulting in a sentence that is approximately five times higher than the guideline range using the base offense level alone. There is an enhancement of at least five levels for distribution, and offenses involving the distribution of material valued at more than $40,000 are enhanced further. A two-level enhancement is provided if the material involved a prepubescent minor or a minor under the age of 12, and a four-level enhancement is added if the material involved sadistic or masochistic conduct or other depictions of violence. A five-level enhancement is provided if the defendant engaged in a pattern of activity involving the sexual abuse or exploitation of a minor. In addition, the commentary in the Application Notes invites an upward departure if the defendant abused a minor at any time.

Thus, under these provisions, if the defendant distributed child pornography that involved a prepubescent child or a child under the age of 12 the offense level would be 22. With a three-level adjustment for acceptance of responsibility, the guideline sentencing range for a first offender would be 30-37 months. However, if the defendant engaged in a pattern of activity involving the sexual abuse or exploitation of a minor, a five-level enhancement would be added to the offense level of 22, making the defendant's offense level 27. With a three-level acceptance of responsibility adjustment, the guidelines would call for a sentence of between 51-63 months.

During 1994 and 1995, a total of 66 defendants were sentenced under guideline 2G2.2. Sixty-five defendants were so sentenced because they were charged and convicted of offenses referenced directly to this guideline. The remaining defendant was convicted of less serious pornography possession charges but was nevertheless cross-referenced to this guideline from §2G2.4. The average prison sentence for these defendants was 28.5 months. Fifty-four percent of the defendants were sentenced within the guideline range; 20 received a sentence within the first quarter of the range. Approximately 38 percent (n=25) received either a substantial assistance departure (n=10) or some other downward departure (n=15). Five defendants received an upward departure based on prior sexual abuse or sexual exploitation of a minor.

Among the defendants sentenced under the guideline, seven received the enhancement for a pattern of activity involving the sexual abuse or exploitation of a minor. Based upon information in the defendants' case files, the Commission identified 14 cases in which it appears that the pattern of activity adjustment could have been applied but was not. Case review further determined that 8 of the 66 defendants sentenced under this guideline could have been sentenced under the production guideline because they were found in possession of pornographic photographs taken by them for their own personal use.

### b. Amendments implementing Congressional directives

The SCACPA directed the Commission to increase the base offense level for trafficking and receipt offenses by at least two levels and to add a two-level enhancement for the use of a computer in such cases. The Commission carried out this directive and submitted the proposed amendments to Congress on April 30, 1996. Based on the data described above, the Commission does not recommend an increase in the base offense level of more than two levels at this time.

### c. Additional amendment submitted to Congress in 1996 to clarify and expand the "pattern of activity" adjustment

Under §2G2.2(b)(4), a defendant sentenced under the trafficking/receipt guideline who engaged in a "pattern of activity involving the sexual abuse or exploitation of a minor" would receive a five-level enhancement. A review of case files, hotline calls, and appellate case law shows that this enhancement is being interpreted inconsistently. Questions arise regarding the scope of the pattern of activity that is to be considered (*i.e.*, does it include prior convictions or only unconvicted activity? is it limited to behavior within the relevant conduct for the offense of conviction or can it include conduct from many years ago?) Other questions involve the meaning of the terms "sexual abuse" and "sexual exploitation."

Most courts appear to give the enhancement only if the defendant had a pattern of sexually abusing a minor or actually exploiting a minor through taking pictures or filming videotapes. However, case analysis shows that courts do not always make the adjustment even in cases involving repeated sexual abuse. On the other hand, at least one court made the adjustment on the basis of repeated trading of pornographic pictures. The defendant appealed application of the adjustment to the First Circuit, which held that the term "sexually exploited" as used in §2G2.2 does not include the computer transmission of child pornography. In addition, the court held that the pattern of activity must relate to the offense of conviction. Thus, prior convictions or uncharged incidents of sexual abuse cannot alone trigger the enhancement. United States v. Chapman, 60 F.3d 894 (1st Cir. 1995).

In response to the second part of this ruling and other evidence of inconsistent and overly limited application of the adjustment, the Commission sent Congress an amendment to clarify the meaning of "pattern of activity" and ensure increased punishment for all offenders who engage in a pattern of sexual exploitation of children. This amendment is discussed in Section G below.

### d. Amendments currently under consideration by the Commission

#### i. Clarify the definition of "distribution" of pornography

The current trafficking/receipt guideline includes a five-level increase if the offense involved distribution. Application Note 1 states that " 'Distribution,' as used in this guideline, includes any act related to distribution for pecuniary gain, including production, transportation, and possession with intent to distribute." It is unclear whether Application Note 1 was intended to limit distribution to acts of a pecuniary nature, and the Department of Justice reports that the application note is sometimes read as being inapplicable to non-pecuniary distribution. Many cases sentenced under this guideline involve trading clubs or other barter types of exchanges. Section G below discusses a change the Commission is considering to provide that both distribution for money and non-pecuniary distribution should receive the five-level enhancement.

#### ii. Consolidate the trafficking/receipt and possession guidelines

Based on our review of child pornography cases sentenced under the guidelines, there appears to be little difference in the offense seriousness between typical receipt cases and typical possession cases. Indeed, all material that is possessed must at some point have been received (unless it was produced, in which case the defendant would be sentenced under the more severe production guideline). It appears that whether the defendant is charged with receipt or possession depends in part on the investigation techniques used to make the case. For example, receipt is easily proven in "sting" cases, but only possession may be provable as a result of a search based on information from a confidential informant. Current statutes and guidelines, however, require that receipt cases be sentenced under the trafficking/receipt guideline, which has a BOL two levels higher than the possession guideline. The following is an example of a receipt case sentenced under the trafficking/receipt guideline.

> ***Case 227339.*** *The defendant responded to an advertisement placed in* The Kinky Marketplace *by a U.S. Postal inspector. The defendant requested a tape depicting one hour of incest and forwarded a blank tape and $80. The undercover inspector sent a return letter asking for verification that the defendant was not an undercover officer as well as the type of "action" in which he was interested. The defendant said he was interested in family incest between parents and their children, and described in explicit detail the sort of sexual scenes he wanted to see. A controlled delivery was made to the defendant's home. After the defendant removed the package from his mail box and carried it inside, the U.S. Postal inspectors executed a search warrant at the residence. Inspectors found the tape in addition to literature and photographs of bestiality and literature on incest. Offense level 14 (BOL 15, +2 for minors under 12, -3 for acceptance of responsibility). Defendant had no criminal record. Final sentence 15 months, bottom of the guideline range.*

The Commission reported concern about the disparity in receipt and possession sentences in 1991 when we amended the guidelines so that receipt cases would be sentenced under the possession guideline. As discussed below in Section G, Congress overrode that amendment and directed the Commission to amend the guidelines so that receipt offenses were sentenced under the trafficking guideline, which has a base offense level two levels higher than the possession guideline.

Based on information in the presentence reports reviewed for this study, it appears that there still may be unwarranted disparity in sentences received for similar conduct and that judges have sought to avoid that disparity in some cases. For example, two cases were "referenced" from the receipt to the possession guideline, even though such a cross reference does not exist, suggesting that judges may have sought to avoid the more severe sentences applicable when a defendant is charged with receipt for conduct that is more like possession than trafficking. Only one case sentenced under the trafficking/receipt guideline was cross referenced from the simple possession guideline, whereas 19 cases sentenced under the possession guideline appear to have been eligible for such a cross reference.

In light of these considerations, the Commission is considering an amendment to consolidate the trafficking/receipt and possession guidelines, a recommendation that is discussed more fully in Section G below.

### 5. Possession Guideline 2G2.4

#### a. Analysis of sentences imposed

Guideline 2G2.4 was created in response to the Crime Control Act of 1990, which defined the possession of more than three items of child pornography as a federal offense. The guideline has a base offense level of 13 and a two-level enhancement if the material involves a prepubescent minor or a minor under age 12. There is an additional two-level increase if the offense involves possessing ten or more books, magazines, or other items depicting the sexual exploitation of a minor, thereby making the adjusted offense level equal to the base offense level of the trafficking/receipt guideline. Additionally, the guideline allows the court to sentence a defendant convicted of possession of child pornography under the more severe trafficking/receipt or production guidelines when warranted.

During 1994 and 1995, 24 defendants were sentenced under guideline 2G2.4. The average prison sentence for these defendants was 15.4 months. Seventy-five percent of the defendants were sentenced within the guideline range; half of these received a sentence within the first quarter of the range. Twenty-five percent (n=6) received a substantial assistance departure (n=3) or other downward departure (n=3). No defendants received an upward departure.

Information in the case files suggests that 19 of the 22 defendants (86 percent) sentenced under the possession guideline may have been more appropriately sentenced under the trafficking/receipt guideline.[9] Offense conduct typically included the receipt of pornography as well as its possession. In fewer cases, the defendant also used the mail to express an interest in receiving child pornography.

#### b. Amendments implementing Congressional directives

The SCACPA directed the Commission to increase the base offense level for child pornography possession offenses by at least two levels and to add a two-level enhancement for the use of a computer in such cases. The Commission carried out this directive and submitted the proposed amendments to Congress on April 30, 1996. The Commission does not recommend any

---

[9] In five of these cases the offenders got a two-level increase for possessing ten or more items of child pornography. This means that they received an offense level of 15, which is the base offense level of the trafficking/receipt guideline to which they could have been referenced. Under the trafficking/receipt guideline, offenders are also exposed to additional upward adjustments not available in the possession guideline.

additional amendments at this time based on the data described above and because of the possibility that some possession sentences may increase if the Commission decides to consolidate the trafficking/receipt and possession guidelines. As described below in Section G, the consolidation of the trafficking/receipt and possession guidelines would make several additional increased punishments available in possession cases, such as the two-level upward adjustment for sadomasochistic material and the five-level upward adjustment for a "pattern of activity" involving the exploitation of a minor.

### 6. The use of substantial assistance motions in child pornography sentencing

Policy statement 5K1.1 and its statutory counterpart, 18 U.S.C. § 3553(e), codify the public policy decision that defendants who assist the government may receive a sentence lower than that called for by the otherwise applicable statutory minimum and guideline range. An otherwise qualifying defendant does not receive the sentence reduction unless the government makes a motion to the court requesting a departure from the guidelines or mandatory minimum. After the government makes the motion, the court must decide whether to reduce the defendant's sentence and how much of a reduction to make.

The SCACPA directs the Commission to "provide an analysis of the type of assistance that courts have recognized as warranting a downward departure from the sentencing guidelines" based on the defendant providing substantial assistance in the prosecution of other persons. The Commission's monitoring data reveal that 15 of 122 cases sentenced pursuant to the pornography guidelines in 1994 and 1995 received such departures. The Commission conducted telephone interviews with federal prosecutors involved in these cases.

Among the benefits from substantial assistance departures that were noted by the government in our interviews were production of physical evidence, identification of other people involved in the production or trafficking of child pornography, new information of trafficking or production in other districts, and other investigative assistance. The most frequent type of cooperation provided by defendants was debriefing the government fully on the criminal activities of others involved in the offense or in similar kinds of misconduct. In one particular case, the defendant, who pleaded guilty to production of child pornography, named five other men who were also involved in the scheme. He also took agents to a warehouse where they discovered the largest cache of child pornography ever seized in the United States. After the other men involved in the production ring learned of the defendant's cooperation, they all pleaded guilty.

In several cases involving the use of computer bulletin boards, the prosecutors told of defendants who would work with agents by going on-line and "talking" to others interested in child pornography. The defendants' computer expertise and knowledge of the child pornography industry, coupled with their willingness to educate the agents, was a tremendous help to the government. Several defendants who were convicted of receipt of child pornography provided the government with names and information about others involved in receiving or distributing child pornography. This information led to referrals, in many instances, to other federal districts where subsequent prosecutions occurred.

Prosecutors commented favorably on the defendants' decisions to cooperate early in the investigation. On numerous occasions, the prosecutors stated that a defendant began to cooperate immediately after arrest. Often, the cooperation began before the defendant retained counsel. All the defendants receiving the departure agreed to testify against someone else, although none of the defendants actually testified. Prosecutors indicated that the testimony was not necessary in many of the cases because the other defendants pleaded guilty as a result of the early cooperation.

Many of the prosecutors interviewed spoke enthusiastically about the law enforcement benefits of substantial assistance. The prosecutors' responses support the viewpoint that §5K1.1 is an effective tool in helping ferret out those who engage in the trafficking or production of child pornography. However, it appears that only a few defendants convicted of child pornography offenses provide this type of assistance.

In summary, (1) few defendants convicted of trafficking or production of child pornography received substantial assistance departures; (2) the defendants' assistance in many of these cases consisted of debriefing prosecutors or agents about others who engaged in similar misconduct; and (3) the defendants' cooperation in most of the cases benefitted the government greatly by leading to other arrests and prosecutions of people involved in the trafficking and production of child pornography.

## C. TRANSPORTATION

### 1. Statutory provisions

Several statutory provisions concern the promotion of prostitution or other prohibited sexual conduct involving a minor. Because federal jurisdiction outside of federally controlled lands hinges on the presence of interstate or international commerce, these statutes involve transportation, travel, or coercion or inducement to travel. Jurisdiction may hinge, as in 18 U.S.C. § 2422(b) recently added by the Telecommunications Act of 1996, on the use of a means of commerce such as the mail or the Internet to induce or coerce a minor to participate in prostitution or other prohibited sexual activity. The statute proscribes "any sexual activity for which any person can be charged with a criminal offense" so long as a basis for federal jurisdiction can be shown.

Thus, the range of conduct covered by these statutes is unusually broad. It includes conduct that is subject to prosecution under different statutes if it occurs within the maritime or territorial jurisdiction of the United States. Thus, rape, sexual abuse of a minor, and other offenses that are the subject of other guidelines may be prosecuted under these jurisdiction-based statutes.

The guideline applicable to these statutes, §2G1.2, uses multiple cross references so courts may use different guidelines to sentence for the underlying criminal conduct. This helps to ensure proportionate punishment among offenders convicted under different statutes whose conduct is in fact similar. These cross-references to other guidelines have, however, resulted in some complexity and they have implications for the implementation of the SCACPA, as discussed below.

## 2. Transportation Guideline 2G1.2

### a. Analysis of sentences imposed

Guideline 2G1.2 serves two functions. First, it is the sentencing guideline for offenses involving the transportation or coercion of minors for purposes of prostitution. The base offense level and specific offense characteristics are geared to reflect this conduct.

Second, the guideline serves a "routing" function. Since the jurisdiction-based statutes indexed to the guideline cover a broad range of conduct, cross references in the guideline allow the court to sentence the defendant under the most appropriate guideline for the underlying offense. The statutes involve both prostitution *and other prohibited sexual conduct.* The cross references are designed to route the non-prostitution cases to the guideline that best reflects this underlying conduct.

Guideline 2G1.2 has a base offense level of 16. An enhancement of four levels is provided if the offense involved the use of physical force or coercion. The guideline also provides a four-level enhancement if the victim is under 12, and a two-level enhancement if the victim is at least 12 but has not attained the age of 16. An additional two-level enhancement is provided if the defendant was a parent, relative, or legal guardian of the minor involved in the offense, or if the minor was otherwise in the custody, care, or supervisory control of the defendant. A Special Instruction is included to treat each person transported as if contained in a separate count of conviction. Application Note 1 also instructs that multiple counts involving the transportation of different persons are not to be grouped together under §3D1.2, thereby ensuring that incremental punishment is provided.

Thus, if the defendant was transporting a minor, age 13, for purposes of prostitution and physical force was used, the offense level would be 22. With a three-level adjustment for acceptance of responsibility, the guideline range for a first offender would be 30-37 months. If the defendant's actual offense conduct included transportation of four minors between the ages of 12 and 16 and physical force was evident, the defendant's offense level would be 26. With the same acceptance adjustment, the guideline range for a first offender would be 46-57 months.

During 1994 and 1995, 10 defendants were sentenced under guideline 2G1.2. The average prison sentence was 44.1 months. Seven defendants were sentenced within the guideline range; three received a sentence within the first quarter of the range. One received a substantial assistance departure and two received other downward departures. No defendant received an upward departure.

*Case 229798. A police sergeant investigating the status of four runaway juvenile girls, ages 13-16, discovered that they had left the state with the defendant. After locating and interviewing the juveniles, police determined that the defendant arranged for the victims to perform sexual activities with adult males. The defendant took advantage of the victims' status as runaways to persuade them that prostitution was a means to obtain money. Offense level was 19 (BOL 16, +2 for victims under 16, + 4 for four victims, - 3 for acceptance of responsibility). Given criminal history Category IV, the Court imposed a final sentence of 57 months in a range of 46-57 months.*

### b. Amendments implementing Congressional directives

In response to a congressional directive under the SCACPA, the Commission has submitted to Congress an amendment to provide a three-level increase in the base offense level for offenses under 18 U.S.C. § 2423(a). Based on the data described above, the Commission does not recommend any additional amendments at this time.

## D. CRIMINAL SEXUAL ABUSE

### 1. Statutory provisions

Federal sexual abuse crimes range from offensive sexual touching to forcible rape. The maximum statutory penalties range from six months imprisonment to life imprisonment. The Commission has promulgated four guidelines to cover these offenses, guidelines 2A3.1-2A3.4. Defendants convicted of federal pornography or transportation offenses whose underlying conduct included sexual abuse are also subject to sentencing under the sexual abuse guidelines via cross references.

Federal statutes divide sexual abuse crimes into aggravated sexual abuse, 18 U.S.C. § 2241, abusive sexual contact, 18 U.S.C. § 2242, and sexual abuse of a minor, 18 U.S.C. § 2243. These provisions were codified as part of the Sexual Abuse Act of 1986. The aggravated sexual abuse statute, 18 U.S.C. § 2241, and the sexual abuse statute, 18 U.S.C. § 2242, prohibit engaging in sexual acts in the special maritime and territorial jurisdiction of the United States or a federal prison. The key distinction between these two provisions lies in the means used to commit the crime; *i.e.* the degree of force or coercion that is used.

The aggravated sexual abuse statute, 18 U.S.C.§ 2241, proscribes knowingly causing another person to engage in a sexual act by using force against that other person or by threatening or placing the other person in fear that any person will be killed, seriously injured, or kidnaped. Aggravated sexual abuse can also, however, be committed in ways that do not include using force or threats. Subsection (b) of the statute punishes (1) knowingly rendering a person unconscious and thereby engaging in a sexual act with that person or (2) administering a drug or some other intoxicant that substantially impairs the ability of the other person to appraise or control conduct and engaging in a sexual act with that person. In addition, § 2241 makes it an offense to knowingly engage in a sexual act with a person under 12 years of age. Attempts to commit any of these acts are also prohibited by the statute. Aggravated sexual abuse is punished by a fine and up to life imprisonment.

The sexual abuse statute, 18 U.S.C. § 2242, punishes those who knowingly (1) cause another person to engage in a sexual act by threatening or placing that other person in fear (other than that proscribed in the aggravated sexual abuse statute) or (2) engage in a sexual act with another person who is (a) incapable of appraising the nature of the conduct or (b) physically incapable of declining participation in, or communicating an unwillingness to engage in, the sexual act. Attempts to commit any of these acts is also prohibited. Sexual abuse is punished by a fine and up to 20 years imprisonment.

The sexual abuse of a minor statute, 18 U.S.C. § 2243(a), applies to behavior in which participants engage without force or threat. The statute proscribes knowingly engaging in a sexual act, or attempting to engage in an act, with another person who (1) is between 12 and 16 years of age, and (2) is at least four years younger than the defendant. The statutory maximum imprisonment penalty was 5 years until 1990 when Congress raised it to 15 years. Section 2243(b) applies to convictions for criminal sexual abuse of a "person in official custody." The statutory maximum penalty is one year. No cases convicted under this provision in the past two years involved children, so the sexual abuse of a ward guideline has been excluded from this analysis.

In addition to these provisions proscribing "sexual acts," 18 U.S.C. § 2244 proscribes conduct involving "sexual contact." "Sexual contact" is defined in § 2246 as the "intentional touching either directly or through the clothing, of the genitalia, anus, groin, breast, inner thigh, or buttocks of any person with an intent to abuse, humiliate, harass, degrade, or arouse or gratify the sexual desire of any person."[10] The penalties for violating the sexual contact statute depend on the same distinctions found in the statutes for sexual acts: ten years imprisonment if the means used would violate § 2241;[11] three years imprisonment if the means used would violate § 2242; two years imprisonment if the conduct would violate § 2243(a); and six months imprisonment if the conduct would violate § 2243(b). Thus, sexual contact is punished less severely than sexual acts, but the same distinctions in culpability, based on the means used and the age or status of the victim, apply to contact as well as to acts.

The Violent Crime Control and Law Enforcement Act of 1994 doubled the statutory penalties for a defendant who violates the provisions of 18 U.S.C. §§ 2241-2243 and who has one or more prior federal or state convictions relating to aggravated sexual abuse, sexual abuse, or abusive sexual contact.[12]

---

[10] 18 U.S.C. § 2246(3) (1994).

[11] The maximum penalty was raised from 5 years to 10 years in 1988.

[12] 18 U.S.C. § 2247 (1994).

Because of the limited federal jurisdiction over these types of offenses, few sexual abuse cases are prosecuted in the federal courts. In 1994 and 1995 only 370 defendants were sentenced in federal court for sexual abuse crimes. Of these, 322 were sentenced under U.S.C. §§ 2241-2244. Children were the victims in 285 (88.5%) of the 322 cases. This analysis examines the sentencing practices in these 285 cases.

2.  **Analysis of sentences imposed under Aggravated Sexual Abuse Guideline 2A3.1**

Guideline 2A3.1 has a base offense level of 27 and represents sexual abuse as set forth in 18 U.S.C. § 2242. An enhancement of four levels is provided for use of force, threat of death, serious bodily injury, kidnaping or certain other means as defined in 18 U.S.C. § 2241(a) or (b). This includes any use or threatened use of a dangerous weapon. [13]

Several other specific offense characteristics, ranging from two- to four-level increases, are provided to account for victims younger than 16, for victim abduction, and for various degrees of victim injury. When a victim is entrusted to the defendant, whether temporarily or permanently, a two-level enhancement applies. The commentary to §2A3.1 states that the enhancement for victimizing a person in the custody, care, or supervisory control of the defendant is to be applied broadly. Teachers, day care providers, babysitters, or other temporary caretakers are examples of those who would be subject to this enhancement.

The guideline directs the court to sentence a defendant under the first-degree murder guideline (base offense level 43) if the victim was killed under circumstances that would constitute murder under the federal murder statute (18 U.S.C. § 1111) had the offense occurred within the federal territorial or maritime jurisdiction of the United States. In response to the Violent Crime Control and Law Enforcement Act of 1994, the Commission added commentary encouraging upward departures (1) if the victim was abused by more than one participant, or (2) if the defendant's criminal history includes a prior sentence for conduct similar to the instant offense.

Thus, if the defendant committed forcible sexual abuse of a child less than 12, the offense level would be 35. A three-level downward adjustment for acceptance of responsibility would lead to a sentencing range of 121-151 months. This sentencing range thus requires a sentence of at least 10 years and one month of imprisonment for a first offender, unless the court finds factors justifying a downward departure. In one of the most serious child sex crimes contemplated, abduction and rape of a child under 12 in the custody, care, or supervisory control of the defendant, where the victim suffers permanent or life threatening injury, the offense level for a first-time offender would be 45. With a three-level downward adjustment for acceptance of responsibility, the defendant's sentencing range would be 360 months to life imprisonment.

Analysis of the 150 cases sentenced under §2A3.1 in both 1994 and 1995 reveals that 130 (87%) involved victims under the age of 18. Of the 130 cases with child victims, sentencing

---

[13] USSG §2A3.1, comment. (backg'd.).

information is available on 117 cases. Based on these 117 cases, the average sentence for defendants sentenced under this guideline for offenses that involved a child victim was 130.4 months.

Because federal jurisdiction for sexual offenses is limited to the territorial and maritime jurisdiction of the United States, 82% of offenders sentenced under this guideline are Native Americans. The ages of the child victims in these cases ranged from 4 years to 17 years, with an average just under 9 years. An "age of the victim" sentence enhancement was made in 119 cases. When the offense conduct began, 23 of the victims were younger than 12 and 96 of the victims were between the ages of 12 and 16. In 120 cases (92%), the victim knew the defendant. In 73 cases (56%), the victim was in the care, custody, or supervisory control of the victim. Several of the defendants were either the father, uncle, or other relative of the defendant. Sixty-nine defendants (53%) were either alcoholics or drug abusers. In 27 cases (21%), there was more than one victim.

Thirty-eight (32.5%) of the defendants were sentenced outside of the guideline range. In one case the court made an upward departure based on the inadequacy of the criminal history score. In three cases the defendants received a downward departure for providing substantial assistance to the government. In the remaining 34 cases (30%), defendants received downward departures for other mitigating reasons, including pursuant to plea agreement (15 cases) and diminished capacity (4 cases). The average sentence for defendants receiving downward departures was 79.6 months.

Of the 79 cases sentenced within the guideline range, 36 defendants were sentenced in the lowest quarter of the guideline range. The remaining defendants were sentenced as follows: 17 in the second quarter, 6 in the third quarter, and 20 in the highest quarter.

Eighty-seven defendants were in Criminal History Category I, with 13 in Criminal History Category II, 16 in Category III, and 14 in Categories IV, V, or VI. Twenty-three defendants (18%) had prior convictions for sexual offenses. A sample of 17 cases was also examined to determine if the defendant had engaged in an ongoing pattern of victimization. Of these, 10 defendants were found to have engaged in such a pattern. An example of one such case follows.

> **Case 193462.** *On October 31, 1992, the victim (age 13) was raped by her cousin's stepfather (age 41) on an Indian reservation. Present were the defendant, his wife and a stepdaughter. The defendant purchased liquor and gave it to his wife who mixed large drinks for her daughter and niece. After the victim drank, she was intoxicated and passed out in a chair. The defendant's wife suggested that her daughter go to a dance at the recreation center. The victim sat inebriated in the chair and the defendant's wife passed out on the floor. The defendant grabbed the victim by the arm, carried her to his bedroom, removed her pants and forcibly had intercourse. The victim told him to stop and attempted to push him off, but the defendant overpowered her. It was later revealed that, in the past, the defendant had repeatedly raped both of his stepdaughters (the youngest was 12 at the time of the offense). Between the time of indictment and trial, the youngest stepdaughter*

*was called to testify when she revealed she had been raped four times by the defendant. The offense level was determined to be 40. (§2A3.1: BOL 27, +4 for use of force, +2 for victim in custody, care or supervisory control of the defendant, +2 for victim between the ages of 12 and 16, +2 for obstruction of justice, +3 for multiple count unit adjustment). Defendant had a criminal history category of I and a guideline range of 292 to 365 months. The defendant was sentenced to 300 months.*

The sexual abuse guidelines have the highest downward departure rate in the guideline system.[14] Thirty percent of defendants receive downward departures for reasons other than substantial assistance. A large percentage of cases sentenced within the guideline range are sentenced within the lowest quarter of the range. In addition, as discussed in the following sections, many cases sentenced under other guidelines with lower BOLs appear to include elements of aggravated sexual abuse.

There are many possible reasons why cases which include elements of aggravation are not always sentenced under the most applicable guideline or given the most severe possible sentence. Some reasons relate to the difficulty of obtaining convictions under these statutes (discussed more fully in section D.3.b.i below). Some prosecutors and judges may be reluctant to impose the full severity of the sexual abuse guideline because the resulting sentences appear too harsh for the unusually complex offense situations typical of federal sexual abuse cases. Some cases of sexual abuse may include factors not adequately taken into account by the guideline structure or may involve combinations of factors that mitigate the offense.

For example, many offenders sentenced for sexual abuse crimes in federal court suffer from substance abuse (36%, n=103) or mental illness (13%, n=38) or both (17%, n=47). Often the offender and victim are intoxicated at the time of the sexual conduct. In federal sexual crimes the victim and offender generally know each other (91%, n=258). Many times they are related either directly or through an extended family circumstance. Exposure of the abuse may have exacted a heavy toll on the family, and incarceration for very long periods of time may appear counterproductive to the court. These and other reasons, discussed more fully below, make it difficult to mandate that practitioners seek the harshest possible punishment in all cases.

3. **Sexual Abuse of a Minor Guideline 2A3.2**

    a. **Analysis of sentences imposed**

---

[14] *See* U.S. SENTENCING COMMISSION, 1995 ANNUAL REPORT 92, Table 32.

The sexual abuse of a minor guideline is intended to be applied to sexual acts involving minors aged 12 to 16 years that would be lawful but for the age of the victim. The base offense level is 15. A two-level increase is provided if the victim was in the custody, care, or supervisory control of the defendant. By cross-reference, the guideline directs the court to sentence a defendant convicted of statutory rape under the more severe aggravated sexual abuse guideline, §2A3.1, if the defendant's conduct would meet the more serious definitions of rape in 18 U.S.C. §§ 2241 or 2242. Commentary to §2A3.2, identical to that in §§2A3.1 and 2A3.4, encourages an upward departure if the defendant's criminal history includes a prior sentence for conduct similar to the instant offense.

> *Case 174221. The female victim, age 14, had intercourse on several occasions with the defendant, age 27, while babysitting his children. The victim stated that she was babysitting for the defendant's children while the defendant and his wife went out drinking. Later that evening, the victim put the children to bed and fell asleep on the couch in the living room. At approximately 2 a.m. the defendant returned home alone and woke her up by kissing her. He then told her to go into his wife's bedroom with him. Once in the bedroom, the defendant removed his clothes and told the victim to do the same. She complied and they both got into bed and had intercourse. The victim said two similar incidents took place a month later. The offense level was determined to be 20 (§2A3.2 BOL 15, +2 for obstruction of justice charge added by judge, not PSR, and +3 for multiple count unit adjustment). Defendant had a Criminal History Category IV and a guideline range of 51-63 months. The defendant was sentenced to 60 months.*

The victim in each of the 52 cases sentenced under this guideline in both 1994 and 1995 was a child between 7 and 16 years old, with an average age of 13.2 years. In 4 of the cases, the victim was less than 12 years old when the conduct began. The victim was in the custody, care or supervisory control of the defendant in 16 of the cases. In most cases (92%) only one victim was involved.

In 41 cases (79%), the defendant was sentenced within the guideline range. Of these 41 cases, 14 were sentenced in the first (lowest) quarter of the guideline range. The remaining defendants were sentenced as follows: 11 in the second quarter, 1 in the third quarter, and 15 in the fourth quarter. In ten of the 52 cases (19%), the defendants received departures. Three defendants received an upward departure resulting in a higher sentence than required by the guidelines. Defendants receiving an upward departure were sentenced to an average of 44 months (range between 36 months and 50 months). Reasons cited for the upward departures included: extreme psychological injury, extreme conduct, general aggravating circumstances, and the on-going nature of the activity.[15] Forty-two cases (81%) were in Criminal History Category I. The average sentence of imprisonment was 21.3 months. Ten (20%) of the defendants had prior convictions for sex offenses.

---

[15] In one case, guideline application information was missing.

None of the defendants sentenced under guideline 2A3.2 received downward departures for substantial assistance. Seven defendants received downward departures for other mitigating reasons. Three defendants receiving downward departures were sentenced to probation. Four cases received prison sentences ranging from 5 to 28 months. The average sentence for these four defendants was 14.0 months. Reasons cited for downward departure included diminished capacity, family ties/responsibilities, isolated incident, and criminal history.

### b. Issues concerning the sexual abuse of a minor guideline

#### i. Non-use of the cross reference to the aggravated sexual abuse guideline

A 1992 Commission study showed that approximately 50 percent of the cases sentenced under §2A3.2 at that time involved aggravated sexual abuse conduct more appropriately punished under §2A3.1.[16] Some cases involved sexual conduct that would be unlawful even if the victim were an adult, such as incest (typically prosecuted under State law; *see also* 18 U.S.C. § 1153), physical force, placing the victim in fear (which is punishable under 18 U.S.C. § 2242), or some other indication of lack of consent on the victim's part. Few of the cases sentenced under the guideline could be termed consensual sexual conduct.

Following the 1992 study, the Commission added a cross reference to §2A3.2 that would direct courts to sentence defendants under the more severe aggravated sexual abuse guideline, 2A3.1. The present analysis indicates, however, that the cross reference is not being used as intended. According to information presented by probation officers in the presentence reports, among the cases sentenced under the guideline, 61 percent involved conduct that could merit a sentence under §2A3.1. In 19 percent of the cases the conduct occurred before the cross reference became available. However, in 42 percent, the cross-reference was available but was not applied. The courts did not use the cross reference in 1994 and 1995.

As noted in the discussion of guideline 2A3.1 above, there are many possible explanations for why cases are being sentenced under a guideline that results in a lower sentence than the guideline that appears most appropriate. Practitioners may perceive that guideline as too severe and seek a sentence that they believe is more appropriate. On the other hand, prosecutors often encounter proof problems in child sexual abuse cases that prevent them from seeking a sentence that would appear to be more appropriate if all relevant conduct were proven at trial or supported by a preponderance of the evidence at sentencing. Among other things, the proof problems could include the strength of the Government's case, the reluctance of witnesses to testify or the determination that a victim may be harmed more by a trial than by a plea agreement. Many sex offenses involve very young victims. Forty-six percent (n=150) of the cases analyzed for this report involve victims under the age of ten years; the abuse may have occurred or begun years before being detected. These victims may not completely recall all the relevant details of the

---

[16] U.S. SENTENCING COMMISSION, CHILD SEX OFFENSE WORKING GROUP REPORT 5 (1992).

abuse, may make for "ineffective" witnesses at trial, or may be further traumatized by a requirement to describe the abuse publicly in court in an adversarial circumstance. Among older victims, issues such as consent, victim intoxication, and unavailability for testimony come into play.

Other reasons, true of sex offenses in general, may help explain why courts do not apply cross references to §2A3.1 from other sex abuse guidelines. Sexual crimes often present the officers of the court with difficult and unusually complex offense situations. These cases present a greater amount of factual "gray area" than the typical federal prosecution. Evidence from hotline calls and case summaries also suggests that practitioners have difficulty interpreting the statutory language of 18 U.S.C. §§ 2241-2242 (aggravated sexual abuse and sexual abuse) which defines the type of force or threatened conduct necessary for the statute and cross reference to apply.

### ii. Increasing punishment for repetitive acts

Some sexual abuse of a minor cases involve a factor that a number of courts believe warrants increased punishment — a repetitive pattern of abuse. In very few instances is the offense a one-time event. Many of the defendants are family members who have access and opportunity to abuse the victim for several years. For example, in United States v. Big Medicine, 73 F.3d 994 (10th Cir. 1995), the defendant was convicted of 18 U.S.C. § 2243(a) and sentenced under §2A3.2 for having sexual intercourse with and impregnating his 15-year-old stepdaughter. In that case, the defendant admitted to having had sex with his stepdaughter on approximately 75 occasions over a period of four years, beginning when the victim was 12 years old. In another case, United States v. Chatlin, 51 F.3d 869 (9th Cir. 1995), the defendant impregnated his 13-year-old stepdaughter. The court sentenced the defendant under §2A3.2 but departed upward on the basis of the defendant's repetitive conduct, extreme conduct and extreme psychological harm to the victim. The appellate court affirmed the reasons given as a basis for the departure, but reversed the district court's decision on the degree of the departure.

In order to ensure that offenses involving repetitive acts are punished sufficiently, the Commission is exploring several options for enhancing sentences based on a pattern of activity involving the sexual exploitation of a minor. These options will be reviewed in Section G below.

### iii. Cases involving incest

According to information presented by probation officers in presentence reports, 45 percent of the cases sentenced under §2A3.2 involved incestuous familial relationships. An additional 53 percent were acquaintance relationships. Just two percent of all cases involved defendants and victims that were neither family nor acquaintances.

Cases involving incest often are sentenced under §2A3.2 because they involve convictions under 18 U.S.C. § 2243(a). The guideline was intended to apply, however, to conduct that would be lawful but for the age of the victim. In United States v. Passi, 62 F.3d 1278 (10th Cir. 1995), the defendant was convicted under 18 U.S.C. § 2243(a) for sexually molesting his biological daughter who became pregnant as a result of the molestation. The court affirmed a cross-reference from guideline 2A3.2 to guideline 2A3.1 on the grounds that the case involved incest, which was not intended to be sentenced under the sexual abuse of a minor guideline since it was not otherwise lawful conduct.

The cases suggest that some incest cases prosecuted under 18 U.S.C. § 2243(a) might be prosecuted under more serious sexual abuse statutory provisions, inasmuch as the offense involves placing the victim in fear. However, if incest cases are appropriately prosecuted under § 2243(a) and sentenced under §2A3.2, it may be that §2A3.2 has not adequately captured the seriousness of this type of offense conduct.

### 4. Analysis of sentences imposed under Abusive Sexual Contact Guideline 2A3.4

The abusive sexual contact guideline punishes conduct that does not involve a sexual act; *i.e.,* no penetration takes place. The guideline has three base offense levels linked to the sections of the statutes that describe degrees of force and coercion. The BOL is 16 for offenses committed by means set forth in 18 U.S.C. § 2241 (a) or (b); *i.e.,* using force or placing the victim in extreme fear or by other extreme coercion, such as involuntary intoxication. The BOL is 12 if the offense is committed by the means set forth in 18 U.S.C. § 2242, *i.e.,* using lesser threats or taking advantage of victims who are incapable of declining participation. The BOL is 10 in other cases that involve consensual acts with minors or wards.

The guideline includes specific offense characteristics regarding the age of the victim. Section 2A3.4(b)(1) provides a four-level enhancement if the victim is under 12, with a minimum offense level of 16. A two-level enhancement is provided under certain circumstances if the victim was age 12 to 16. A two-level enhancement is provided if the victim was in the custody, care, or supervisory control of the defendant. The commentary encourages a six-level downward departure in cases of consensual sexual contact "[i]f the defendant and the victim are similar in sexual experience."[17]

Thus, if a defendant knowingly engaged or caused sexual contact by force with a child under 12, an offense which carries a statutory maximum penalty of 10 years, the offense level would be 20. With a three-level downward adjustment for acceptance of responsibility, the guideline range for a first offender would be 24-30 months.

During 1994-1995, 115 cases were sentenced under §2A3.4. Of these, 103 (90%) had child victims. Sentencing information was available for 101 of these cases. Most of the defendants were either parents or other relatives of the victims. Forty-six of the defendants received the enhancement for having the victim in their care, custody or control. The average age of the victims was nine years old, with ages ranging between 2 and 16 years. Eighteen percent of the cases involved multiple victims.

---

[17] Background Commentary to §2A3.4 recommends an offense level of 6.

The average term of imprisonment was 22 months. Seventy-nine defendants (78%) were sentenced within the guideline range. Of these 79 defendants, 36 were sentenced in the lowest quarter of the guideline range. The remaining defendants were sentenced as follows: 16 in the second quarter, 7 in the third quarter, and 20 in the highest quarter. Two defendants received an upward departure. Reasons cited include: several persons were injured, extreme psychological injury, and on-going abuse. Twenty defendants (20%) received downward departures for cited reasons that included general mitigating factors (4 cases) and their plea agreement (7 cases). None of the defendants received substantial assistance departures. Seventy-eight of the defendants were in Criminal History Category I. Six defendants (6%) had convictions for prior sexual offenses.

Like the sexual abuse of a minor guideline, the abusive sexual contact guideline contains a cross reference, directing the court to sentence under a more severe guideline if the defendant's conduct involves a sexual act and not mere sexual contact. For example, a defendant is to be sentenced under §2A3.1 if the court finds that the defendant's conduct involved penetration, no matter how slight, rather than touching alone. The court must then decide the degree of force involved to determine the appropriate offense level. Sentences for sexual acts involving similar degrees of force or coercion are 15 offense levels higher than for sexual contact alone.

According to information presented by probation officers in presentence reports, in 54 percent of the cases sentenced under the abusive sexual contact guideline, the defendant committed acts that could merit sentencing under the aggravated sexual abuse guideline. Fifteen percent of the cases were sentenced before the cross reference was applicable. In 40 percent of the cases, the conduct was rape and the cross reference could have been used, but it was applied in only four cases. In one case a defendant committed conduct which could be sentenced under the sexual abuse of a minor guideline, §2A3.2, but the cross reference was not applied.

## E. THE USE OF COMPUTERS IN CHILD PORNOGRAPHY DISTRIBUTION

### 1. Ways that computers can be used to disseminate pornography

This section begins by describing the different ways that computers can be used to disseminate child pornography. The problems identified by Congress that led to a call for increased punishment for computer use are identified, and those uses that most exacerbate these problems are described. Finally, ways to tailor punishments to suit the harm caused by different types of computer use are analyzed.

All of the systems described below can be accessed through a personal computer using widely available communications hardware and software. A modem attached to a personal computer gives access via ordinary phone lines directly to other computers or to an online service provider. The provider then gives access to other computers and to the Internet. Once on the Internet, users have access to its many components, including e-mail, Newsgroups, and the World Wide Web. The following glossary gives a basic introduction to these systems and to their potential abuse.

**Online Services (America Online, Compuserve, Prodigy, Microsoft Network, etc.):** These private companies provide subscribers with information services, access to the Internet, and forums for dialogue among subscribers. They expressly prohibit the posting of any sexually explicit images on the company-owned sites. However, members can access the Internet through the service and therefore get material that the online providers cannot regulate. The "private" chat rooms on America Online and Compuserve also provide an avenue for explicit conversation between subscribers. Companies differ concerning the accessability of various services. For example, America Online provides access to the full range of services to each computer/subscriber. Prodigy, however, permits subscribers to define different access rights for different individuals using the same account.

**Bulletin Boards (BBS):** A computer that stores information and provides a means for users at other locations to send and receive files. Bulletin boards preceded public use of the Internet and provided the earliest widespread means of sharing information among computers at different locations through the use of modems and regular phone lines. BBS are created and maintained by individual operators who establish the rules for access and for the types of material that may be posted. Graphic files may be sent and received from BBS. Hundreds of thousands of BBS are currently in operation. Some are "wide open," meaning that the telephone number to gain access is publicly available, no password is required, and there are no subscription fees. Others require paid membership, generally ranging from $10 to $30 a month. Some BBS screen applicants and verify age and other information (driver's license, place of employment, credit cards) before granting access. Most BBS contain harmless information, but a small percentage of "adult" BBS contain pornography. Almost all of these adult BBS require fees and prior membership approval before they can be accessed.

**Electronic Mail (E-Mail ):** Electronically transmitted mail through use of the Internet. Senders must address messages to a particular recipient or group of recipients. Many versions of e-mail software permit the user to attach text, data, sound, or image files when sending a message. Senders must know the exact destination address to use e-mail.

**Newsgroups (primarily known as Usenet):** News groups are self-forming clubs organized by hierarchically indexed topics. Persons with the proper Internet access can browse the list of groups currently in operation, such as alternative sexuality, and read or post messages for any group. To be routinely sent a news group's messages, a user must register with that group. Newsgroups are routing lists for e-mail messages, which can include graphic files in a compressed format.

**World Wide Web (WWW):** A user-friendly, hypermedia system for storing, linking, and accessing information on the Internet. Information is indexed using several search techniques. Web browsers, such as Yahoo, provide information directories linking users to indexed sites. Search engines, such as Netscape, permit searches for particular combinations of words or phrases. Or users can "surf" from one site to another simply by clicking on highlighted phrases that connect to other related sites. Each information site generally contains a homepage that enables users to link to related files to retrieve text, video, graphics and sound. Among the thousands of Websites currently in operation, some are pornography distribution sites. Some sites provide free access to visual images; others provide purchase order forms.

### 2. Public and congressional concerns about pornography and computers

Media coverage in the past year has highlighted the availability of pornography through computers. For example, a cover story in Time Magazine reported a controversial study of "cyberporn" by Carnegie Mellon researchers.[18] The story claimed that "the adult BBS market seems to be driven largely by a demand for images that can't be found in the average magazine rack: pedophilia (nude photos of children), hebephilia (youths) and what researchers call paraphilia -- a grab bag of deviant material . . . ."

Others dispute that child pornography is available by computer through ordinary channels. In response to a notice posted on the Internet as part of the Commission's study, Aliza R. Panitz, a Website administrator and Internet educator replied: "During the extensive research involved in creating and maintaining the AltSex [alternative sexuality] site, we have come across a fair number of adults-only sites containing erotic images, but we have NEVER found a site containing either erotic images of children or child pornography. While there may well be child pornography accessible through the Internet, it is neither visible to the casual viewer nor accessible through standard search techniques for erotic materials."

The SCACPA increases punishment for use of a computer in child pornography offenses. The legislative history of the Act indicates that Congress had identified four concerns: (1) the wide dissemination and instantaneous transmission in computer-assisted trafficking of child pornography, (2) the increased difficulty of investigation and prosecution by law enforcement officials, (3) the increased likelihood that child pornography will be viewed by and harm children, and (4) the potential for pedophiles to lure children into sexual relationships through the computer.[19] By lengthening sentences, Congress aims to punish and deter these crimes and to remove from the community the persons who perpetrate them.

---

[18] Marty Rimm, *Marketing Pornography on the Information Superhighway: A Survey of 917,410 Images, Descriptions, Short Stories, and Animations Downloaded 8.5 Million Times by Consumers in Over 2000 Cities in Forty Countries, Provinces, and Territories*, 83 GEO. L.J. 1849-1934 n. 5 (1995). A detailed analysis of the conceptual and methodological flaws in the Rimm study is found in Donna L. Hoffman and Thomas P. Novak, *A Detailed Analysis of the Conceptual, Logical, and Methodological Flaws in the Article, 'Marketing Pornography on the Information Superhighway'*, Project 2000 Critique, Version 1.01 [www2000.ogsm.vanderbilt.edu/rimm.cgi] (1995).

[19] *See* H.R. REP. NO. 90, 104th Cong., 1st Sess. 3-4 (1995), reprinted in 1996 U.S.C.C.A.N. 759.

3.  **Cyberporn and culpability**

Online pornography comes from the same pool that can be found in specialty magazines or adult bookstores. Most of the material accessible by computer is scanned from existing print publications, using graphic scanners that are available for less than a thousand dollars. Thus, the differences between print and computerized porn is not in the content of the images, but in the means of its distribution. The seriousness of a crime involving computerized trafficking in child pornography depends in part on 1) the degree to which the computer use facilitates the widespread and instantaneous distribution of the images, and 2) the degree to which it increases the likelihood that children will be exposed to the images.

Different types of computer use have different effects on these two harms. "Downloading" cyberporn is similar to receiving pornography through the mail. Although anyone with a mailbox can receive print pornography, a modem and a computer with graphic capability are needed to receive cyberporn.

There are many different uses of computers to send or distribute images. At one end are small-scale collectors who freely give or exchange images with like-minded persons through electronic mail. The advent of computers has probably made the formation of networks of child pornography consumers easier, since such persons can look for each other by "plugging in" to the right chat room, bulletin board, or newsgroup. Once formed, these networks can operate as underground distribution systems.[20]

At the other end are large-scale, commercial pornographers. Creating and maintaining a BBS or Website with pornography is similar to opening an adult bookstore. Unlike adult bookstores, however, which may be limited by zoning laws to particular areas or outlawed altogether, cyberstores may be accessed anywhere a computer can be linked to the Internet, depending on the rules for access to the particular BBS or Website. This accessibility requires that the creators of Websites and publicly accessible BBS be responsible for the potentially greater accessibility of their products. Some locations on the WWW contain pornographic images of adults and are easily accessible to anyone using standard Web Browsers.[21] Some locations give warnings that only persons over 18 should enter, while others do not. As noted above, some BBS screen applicants before granting access, while others are wide open. Persons who upload, send,

---

[20] To attract new members, however, such networks must be visible to some degree, which makes them susceptible to surveillance and sting operations conducted by online law enforcement.

[21] Commercial companies have developed products that are designed to allow computer owners to block access to sites on the Web where pornographic images can be found. The constitutionality of the provisions in the Telecommunications Act of 1995 that prohibit "indecent" communication by computer have been challenged in part based on the availability of such products, which may provide a less restrictive way to regulate such communication.

or post illegal images to accessible sites should be held accountable for the harm done when child pornography is widely disseminated or falls into the hands of children.

While the extent of commercial child pornography distribution through computer networks is a matter of dispute, what seems apparent is that a person's culpability depends on *how* they use a computer. Persons who receive images are similar to consumers of print porn who receive packages from acquaintances or go to bookstores to buy dirty magazines. Persons who transmit the images, however, may be mailing a single photo to a friend, or they may be more similar to a person who opens an adult bookstore in every city in the world. Not all computer use is equal. Some uses lead to more widespread dissemination of child pornography and to increased accessibility of pornography and other sexually explicit dialogue to children. Sentencing policy should be sensitive to these differences in culpability so that punishments are tailored to fit the circumstances of each individual's crime.

### 4. Computer use among federal pornography defendants

Federal cases to date typically do not involve the type of computer use that would result in either wide dissemination or a likelihood that the material will be viewed by children. Of the 22 cases sentenced under §2G2.1, the production guideline, four involved the use of a computer. In two of these cases, the use was limited to the storage of forms (not pornographic images) related to the pornography. In one case, the defendant used the computer to contact another individual interested in child pornography and invited this person to join the defendant and several teenage victims in sexual misconduct. In the remaining case, the computer was used to possess, receive, distribute, and create or enhance images. Additionally, this defendant posted notices on the availability of child pornography and maintained records.

Of the 66 cases sentenced under §2G2.2, the trafficking/receipt guideline, 22 involved the use of a computer. A broad array of computer involvement was found. In some cases, computers were used only to store the pornographic images. In another case, a defendant stored and received the images by computer, posted notices of interest in receiving and sending child pornography, enhanced the images, and distributed the pornography for profit and with the belief that minors would be among the recipients. Of these 22 cases, 17 involved acts of distribution, seven of which were for profit. In nine of the 22 cases, defendants posted notices of interest in receiving child pornography, and in four cases defendants posted notices regarding the availability of child pornography.

Of the 24 cases sentenced under §2G2.4, the possession guideline, nine involved the use of a computer to store or receive the pornographic images.

In summary, of the 112 child pornography cases reviewed for this study, 35 involved the use of a computer. Of these computer cases, 17 involved defendants who had received pornographic images, generally from a BBS. Another 17 cases involved distribution by computer. About half of these cases involved e-mailing a pornographic image to a single recipient, while the other half involved creating or maintaining a BBS from which child pornographic images could be downloaded.[22]

### 5. Punishing the use of computers to spread child pornography

The SCACPA directed the Commission to add enhancements to the guidelines "[1] if a computer was used to transmit the notice or advertisement to the intended recipient or [2] *to transport or ship the visual depiction*" (emphasis added). Amendments sent to Congress on April 30, which add a two-level upward adjustment in cases involving a computer, track this statutory language. This adjustment applies to persons who knowingly receive e-mail containing pornographic images, as well as to those who send the images.[23] The adjustment does not distinguish between persons who e-mail images to a single voluntary recipient and those who establish a BBS and distribute child pornography to large numbers of subscribers.

Congress and the Commission may wish to develop a more finely-tuned system of apportioning punishment in cases involving the use of computers. For example, an upward departure might be recommended in cases in which a computer was used to widely disseminate pornography, or in which pornography was made accessible to children. Alternatively, the two-level adjustment might be narrowed to apply only to cases that involve distributing child pornography in a way that makes it widely accessible, such as posting it on a BBS or Website. However, a statutory amendment may be necessary to make these kinds of distinctions because the current statutory directive is aimed broadly at all persons who use a computer to transmit child porn, including receivers and possessors.

The uses of computers are evolving rapidly. Though the overall numbers remain small, the portion of federal child pornography cases that involved computers grew between 1994 (23%) and 1995 (28%). The Commission intends to closely monitor the variety of computer uses in pornography distribution and amend the guidelines as appropriate.

---

[22] One case involved the use of a computer to solicit a person to actually engage in sexual acts with minors.

[23] As reported out of the House Committee on the Judiciary, the computer enhancement did not apply to possession offenses. Section 3 of the bill was amended in the Senate to provide the two-level enhancement for possession offenses under section 2252(a)(4), as well as to trafficking offenses under sections 2251(c)(1)(A) and 2252(a)(1) through (3). No legislative history explaining the concerns motivating this amendment is available. The proposed guideline amendment to the possession guideline §2G2.4 limits the adjustment to cases in which the defendant's possession resulted from the defendant's use of the computer.

## F. TARGETING DANGEROUS OFFENDERS

### 1. The dangers of sex offenses against children

During 1993, there were approximately 150,000 confirmed cases of sexual child abuse in the United States.[24] Studies of the adult population have indicated that at least 20 percent of American women and 5 to 10 percent of American men have been the victims of sexual child abuse.[25] "Most sexual abuse is committed by men (90%) and by persons known to the child (70% to 90%), with family members constituting one-third to one-half of the perpetrators against girls and 10% to 20% of the perpetrators against boys."[26] A review of international studies of child sexual abuse reported findings that are generally consistent with those cited above.[27] Children who have been sexually abused often have higher rates of later childhood and adult mental health symptomatology.[28]

In cases involving the sexual victimization of children, special attention must be paid to identifying those offenders who show the greatest risk of victimizing children in the future, so that they can be provided appropriate treatment or incapacitated through extended imprisonment. The SCACPA requires that the Commission survey the recidivism rate for offenders convicted of committing sex crimes against children, analyze the impact of treatment on recidivism, and determine whether increased penalties might reduce such recidivism.[29]

---

[24]David Finkelhor, *Current Information on the Scope and Nature of Child Sexual Abuse*, 4 FUTURE OF CHILDREN 31-53 (1994).

[25]B. Watkins & A. Bentovim, *The Sexual Abuse of Male Children and Adolescents: A Review of Current Research*, 33 J. CHILD PSYCHOL. & PSYCHIATRY & ALLIED DISCIPLINES 197-248 (1992).

[26]Finkelhor, *supra* note 24, at 31.

[27]David Finkelhor, *The International Epidemiology of Child Sexual Abuse*, 18 CHILD ABUSE & NEGLECT 409-417 (1994).

[28]*See* RONALD M. HOLMES, SEX CRIMES (1991); Finkelhor, *supra* note 27; S. Harter, P.C. Alexander & R.A. Neimeyer, *Long-Term Effects of Incestuous Child Abuse in College Women: Social Adjustment, Social Cognition, and Family Characteristics*, 56 J. CONSULTING AND CLINICAL PSYCHOL. 5-8 (1988); J.A. Bushnell, J.E. Wells & M.A. Oakley-Brown, *Long-term Effects of Intrafamilial Sexual Abuse in Childhood*, 85 ACTA PSYCHIATR. SCAND. 136-142 (1992).

[29]Section 6(4). The General Accounting Office (GAO) has also been tasked by Congress to study child sex abusers and the impact of treatment on recidivism. The Commission has focused on general recidivism and GAO will report on the effectiveness of treatment.

a. **Recidivism among child sexual abusers**

A great deal of scientific literature has been published on the likelihood of sexual re-offending among persons committing sexual offenses. Much of this literature, however, is not conducive to comparisons across studies or straightforward summation of results because of the varied and imprecise study methodologies employed, examples of which include: poorly described subject selection and rejection criteria; poorly (or non-) defined sexual conduct; diverse definitions of recidivism; and varied lengths of follow-up.

Two recent major reviews of the literature on sexual child abuse have been completed. The first review, conducted by Furby and her colleagues, was published in 1989. It examined sexual child abuse research from the 1950s onward.[30] The second major review, focusing on post-treatment recidivism reported since 1989, was published in 1995.[31] In this latter review, Nagayama Hall analyzed 12 scientific studies (from a pool of 92 studies) that met the criteria of a control group, and specifically reporting recidivism for a sexual offense.

The overall recidivism rate across studies among untreated sex offenders was 27 percent. This was compared to a sex offense recidivism rate of 19 percent for offenders who had received treatment related to their sexual misconduct. It is important to note that the range of sexual recidivism in these studies varied widely. The range of recidivism among the untreated offenders varied between 6 and 75 percent, dependent upon the specific study. The range for the treated offenders was between 3 and 44 percent. The average length of follow-up across studies was 6.8 years.[32]

The earlier Furby review, citing the methodological problems described above, did not report overall rates of recidivism. The authors did however cautiously report several suggestive trends from their analysis: "(a) The longer the follow-up period is, the greater is the percentage of men who have committed another crime . . . ; (b) There is as yet no evidence that clinical

---

[30]Lita Furby, *et al.*, *Sex Offender Recidivism: A Review*, 105 PSYCHOL. BULLETIN 3-30 (1989). The authors reviewed 42 primary study sources and 13 secondary sources.

[31]Gordon C. Nagayama Hall, *Sexual Offender Recidivism Revisited: A Meta-Analysis of Recent Treatment Studies*, 63 J. CONSULTING & CLINICAL PSYCHOL. 802-809 (1995).

[32]For purposes of comparison, Harer (1994) examined recidivism of federal prisoners released from the Bureau of Prisons in 1987. He reported that for all offense types combined, 40.8% repeated offenses within a three-year period. In this study, only eight sexual offenders were available for analysis and, of these, four repeated offenses. No information on type of sex crime or type of recidivating event was reported. Because of the small number of cases and lack of more specific information about the offenders, this data on sex offenders should be interpreted very cautiously. MILES D. HARER, RECIDIVISM AMONG FEDERAL PRISON RELEASEES IN 1987: A PRELIMINARY REPORT (Federal Bureau of Prisons, Office of Research and Evaluation, 1994).

treatment reduces rates of sex reoffenses . . . ; [and (c)] There is some evidence that recidivism rates may be different for different types of offenders."[33]

Several authors have noted that a sexual child molester remains at risk of recidivism for very long periods of time.[34] One author, who followed sexual offenders for up to 10 years, reported that "there is no evidence of burn out and risk was as great in the seventh year, for example, as it was in the first."[35]

### b. Commission data on recidivism among federal child sex offenders

Of the 138 cases indexed to the pornography and transportation guidelines, about 20 percent had a prior sex-related conviction. Twenty percent of transportation cases involving prostitution and 13 percent of pornography defendants had a history of sexual misconduct. Higher rates of prior records were found in offenders who were cross-referenced from these guidelines to the sexual abuse guidelines. It appears that *some* defendants sentenced under *each* of the guidelines exhibit a pattern of recidivism.

Among the 285 defendants analyzed under the sexual abuse guidelines, 14 percent (39 cases) had a prior conviction for a sexual offense. In 64 percent of the 39 cases, the prior sex crime was against a child. The rate of sex crime recidivism was about the same for aggravated sexual abuse and sexual abuse of a minor (18% and 19%, respectively) and substantially lower for abusive sexual contact (6%). The likelihood that a child was the prior victim was high for all three guidelines (65% of §2A3.1 sexual recidivists (15 cases), 70% of §2A3.2 sexual recidivists (7 cases), and 50% of §2A3.4 sexual recidivists (3 cases)).

## 2. Current guidelines take multiple approaches to targeting dangerous offenders

The key to wise use of prison resources is to target those offenders who present the greatest risk of continued harm to society for the lengthiest incarceration. The current guidelines adopt varied, and sometimes inconsistent, approaches to this task. The criminal history guidelines in Chapter Four of the *Guidelines Manual* count previous convictions for sex offenses against children just as they count other previous offenses that fall within the rules governing criminal history points.

---

[33]Furby, *et al.*, *supra* note 30 at 27.

[34]*See* Nagayama Hall, *supra* note 31; W.L. Marshall & H.E. Barbaree, *The Long Term Evaluation of a Behavioral Treatment Program for Child Molesters*, 26 BEHAV. RES. THER. 499-511 (1988). *See also*, Robert J. McGrath, *Sex-Offender Risk Assessment and Disposition Planning: A Review of Empirical and Clinical Findings*, 35 INT'L J. OFFENDER THER. & COMP. CRIMINOLOGY 329-350 (1991); and V.L. Quinsey, *et al.*, *Actuarial Prediction of Sexual Recidivism*, 10 J. INTERPERSONAL VIOLENCE 85-105 (1995).

[35]Quinsey, *et al.*, *supra* note 34 at 94.

The criminal sexual abuse guidelines, §§2A3.1-4, take a different approach. An application note in each guideline states that "[i]f the defendant's criminal history includes a prior sentence for conduct that is similar to the instant offense, an upward departure may be warranted." *See, e.g.*, USSG §2A3.1, Application Note 7. In addition, the aggravated sexual abuse guideline recommends an upward departure in cases involving multiple victims or multiple acts with the same victim, if this behavior is not adequately captured by the counts of conviction or by application of the guidelines' grouping rules. *See* USSG §2A3.1, Application Note 5.

The pornography guidelines take several different approaches to recidivist offenders. A five-level upward adjustment for "a pattern of activity involving the sexual abuse of a minor" was added to the trafficking guideline in 1992. However, the courts are applying this adjustment in inconsistent ways. In addition, the Application Notes to the trafficking guideline contain a broad recommendation for an upward departure "[i]f the defendant sexually exploited or abused a minor at any time, whether or not such sexual abuse occurred during the course of the offense . . . ." The pornography production and possession guidelines, however, contain no adjustments or application notes concerning high-risk offenders. As the case analysis shows, high-risk offenders may be convicted and sentenced under any of the pornography guidelines. There appears to be no reason to limit this type of adjustment to the trafficking guideline, as discussed in the recommendations under Section G below.

### 3. Risk classification of child sexual abusers

The development of classification systems for sexual offenders serves two primary purposes: 1) evaluation of the risk of repeat offending, and 2) diagnosis and treatment planning. The most consistent finding is that criminal history, especially a history of sexual offenses, is the most important and accurate predictor of the risk of future sexual offending.[36] This is consistent with research on the prediction of other sorts of recidivism.

In addition to criminal history, sexual offenders can be classified by the characteristics of their victim. Pedophiles are adults who are sexually attracted to children; hebephiles are adults interested in children who are between puberty and adolescence.[37] The scientific literature has indicated two additional victim characteristics that are important in classifying sexual offenders: 1)

---

[36]R. Karl Hanson, *et al.*, *Long-Term Recidivism of Child Molesters*, 61 J. CONSULTING & CLINICAL PSYCHOL. 646-652 (1993). Nearly all of these offenders (93%) were followed for at least 15 years and some were followed for over thirty years. Quinsey *et al.*, *supra* note 34; and Rice, M.E., Quinsey, V.L., Harris, G.T., *Sexual Recidivism Among Child Molesters Released From A Maximum Security Psychiatric Institution*, 59 J. CONSULTING & CLINICAL PSYCHOL. 381-386 (1991).

[37]Holmes, *supra* note 28.

the relationship of the victim to the perpetrator; *i.e.,* whether the abuse is intra-familial or extra-familial, and 2) the gender of the victim.[38]

One long term follow-up study involved 197 child molesters in Canada.[39] In this study, male offenders were classified into three groups based on the characteristics of their victims: extra-familial boys; extra-familial girls; and intra-familial (incest). During the period of follow-up for these offenders, 42 percent were subsequently reconvicted of a sexual offense, a violent offense or both.[40] An important finding was that risk of recidivism varied by group. Offenders against boys were at significantly higher risk of recidivism than incest offenders or offenders against girls. For incest offenders, the recidivism rate was lower than for offenders against extra-familial girls, though not at a statistically significant level.[41] This general pattern of greater risk for extra-familial offenders has been replicated by other researchers, though evidence on the importance of the gender of the victim is inconsistent.[42]

Efforts are under way to extend and improve classification of sexual misconduct through the use of physiologic (*e.g.* phallometric response to erotic stimuli) and psychologic (*e.g.* clinical interview, personality tests, etc.) measures. McGrath (1991) offers a decision tree framework for assessing the risk of sexual recidivism. He includes for consideration a broad array of factors such as: presence of other severe psychopathology (*e.g.* psychosis); presence of substance abuse disorders; use of force or violence; presence of ritualistic or bizarre offenses; denial of current offense; treatment refusal; numbers of victims; presence of other paraphilias; stability of environment; deviant sexual arousal patterns; prior criminal activity (both sexual and non-sexual); etc. He reviews the scientific literature supporting these elements as relevant in a classification

---

[38]The extra-familial versus intra-familial characteristic appears to be the more certain criterion for evaluating risk of recidivism at this time. The literature on the predictive impact of sex of the victim on recidivism, given that the victim is extra-familial, is mixed.

[39]Hanson *et al., supra* note 36. Nearly all of these offenders (93%) were followed for at least 15 years and some were follewed for over 30 years.

[40]In this and other studies examining sexual recidivism, both sexual and violent offenses are generally included in an effort to account for charge bargaining practices. When reporting results, known sexual recidivism and violent recidivism are described separately.

[41]Hanson, *et al., supra* note 36 at 649. The specific rates of recidivism for these offender types was presented only in chart form. It appears that the recidivism rates (and approximate durations of follow-up for these groups), by victim relationship/sex, were: 65% of offenders victimizing extra-familial boys recidivated over a 20 year period; 50% of offenders victimizing extra-familial girls recidivated over a 30 year period; and 25% of incest offenders recidivated over 20 years.

[42]Marshall, *et al., supra* note 34.

model, but a test of the predictive validity has yet to be performed.[43] Likewise, Prentky and colleagues at the Massachusetts Treatment Center are developing classification models for adult rapists that focus on specific elements of the crime and include measures of lifestyle impulsivity in the decision matrix.[44]

Most research on risk-classification is retrospective; that is, it classifies offenders after the recidivating event and attempts to identify differences that were present before the event.[45] Some studies have attempted to make retrospective "predictive" classifications. Rice and colleagues (1991) reported results on the accuracy of a measure (including personal, psychological, criminal and sexual preference characteristics of the offender) on "predicting" recidivism. They reported that 80 percent of the offenders could be correctly classified with this method.[46]

### 4. Implications for sentencing policy

Research should be monitored so that reliable results can be incorporated into sentencing policy. At this time, however, the data are insufficient to base sentencing policy on these methods of classification. Classification tools have two measures of accuracy: 1) sensitivity, *i.e.,* the ability of a tool to avoid "false negative" errors by correctly identifying the persons who *will* recidivate; and 2) specificity, *i.e.,* the ability of a tool to avoid "false positive" errors by correctly excluding persons who *will not* recidivate. Generally, a classification tool performs better either in its sensitivity or specificity. For example, sensitivity can be improved but at the cost of labeling

---

[43]McGrath, *supra* note 34.

[44]Robert A. Prentky, *et al., Predictive Validity of Lifestyle Impulsivity for Rapists*, 22 CRIM. JUST. & BEHAV. 106 (1995); Robert A. Prentky & Raymond A. Knight, *Identifying Critical Dimensions for Discriminating Among Rapists*, 59 J. CONSULTING & CLINICAL PSYCHOL. 643-661 (1991); Robert A. Prentky, *et al., Development of a Rational Taxonomy for the Classification of Rapists: The Massachusetts Treatment Center System*, 13 BULL. AM. ACAD. PSYCHIATRY & L. 39-70 (1985).

[45]*See, e.g.,* Quinsey, *et al., supra* note 34; Hanson *et al., supra* note 36; Rice, *et al., supra* note 36; R. Karl Hanson, *et al., A Comparison of Child Molesters and Nonsexual Criminals: Risk Predictors and Long-Term Recidivism*, 32 J. RES. CRIME & DELINQUENCY 325-337 (1995); Janice Marques, *et al., The Relationship Between Treatment Goals and Recidivism Among Child Molesters*, 32 BEHAV. RES. THER. 577-588 (1994); and Fred S. Berlin & Carl F. Meinecke, *Treatment of Sex Offenders with Antiandrogenic Medication: Conceptualization, Review of Treatment Modalities, and Preliminary Findings*, 138 AM. J. PSYCHIATRY 601 (1981).

[46]Rice *et al., supra* note 36. The authors also a report a statistic which assesses the classification ability of the tool accounting for the chance probability of correct classification. They reported that their measures had a relative improvement over chance of 55%. That is, in a coin toss situation (two outcomes), this instrument would be better than chance 55% of the time. Given an equal probability of outcome (a coin toss), a correct prediction of the result of the toss would occur approximately 78 out of 100 tosses.

some offenders as potential recidivists who would not repeat the crime. Evaluating a classification system depends on the costs associated with the two types of errors.

From an incapacitation perspective, research presently supports targeting for lengthier incarceration those offenders who have a history of prior sexual misconduct against children. The guideline criminal history score is one method for focusing on repeat offenders. In addition, as discussed in the recommendations below, expansion of the "pattern of activity" adjustment now found in the pornography trafficking/receipt guideline would also improve the sensitivity of the guidelines with minimum damage to their specificity.

## G. RECOMMENDATIONS

### 1. Guideline amendments submitted to Congress in 1996

#### a. Amendments implementing Congressional directives

The Commission carried out the congressional directives contained in sections 2, 3, and 4 of the SCACPA by adopting and submitting guideline amendments to Congress on April 30, 1996.[47] In particular, the Commission (1) increased the base offense levels in §§2G2.1, 2G2.2, and 2G2.4 by two levels for offenses under 18 U.S.C. §§ 2251 and 2252, (2) increased the base offense level in §2G1.2 by three levels for offenses under 18 U.S.C. § 2423(a), and (3) provided a two-level enhancement in §§2G2.2 and 2G2.4 for the use of a computer in child pornography trafficking, receipt, and possession cases.

#### b. Additional amendments to improve the guidelines

In addition to implementing the directives contained in the SCACPA, the Commission adopted other amendments in 1996 that were designed to improve the child pornography and transportation guidelines.

##### i. Enhancement for use of a computer to solicit participation in production

In order to punish for the use of a computer more consistently, the Commission added a two-level enhancement in §2G2.1 if a computer was used to solicit participation in sexually explicit conduct by or with a minor for the purpose of producing a visual depiction of that conduct, in violation of 18 U.S.C. § 2251(c)(1)(B). Thus, persons who induce minors to participate in the production of pornography through computerized "chat rooms" or by using e-mail will receive longer sentences. Increased punishment is justified because of the additional harm caused by the use of a computer to lure children into sexual relationships.

---

[47] Amendments to the Sentencing Guidelines for United States Courts, 61 Fed. Reg. 20,306 (1996).

### ii. Clarification of "pattern of activity" adjustment

In order to better ensure lengthy incarceration for those offenders who are the most likely to commit new sex crimes, the Commission revised the application note in commentary to §2G2.2(b)(4), which provides a five-level enhancement if the defendant engaged in a "pattern of activity involving the sexual abuse or exploitation of a minor." The revision clarifies that the pattern of activity may include acts of sexual abuse or exploitation that are proven to the court at sentencing, even if the acts were not committed during the course of the offense or did not result in a conviction. The revision also clarifies that the defendant must have personally engaged in sexual abuse or exploitation. For example, repeated mailings of pornography do not constitute a pattern of abuse or exploitation for purposes of this adjustment. The commentary was also revised to specify that an upward departure may be appropriate in some cases in which the pattern of activity adjustment does not apply or does not adequately reflect the seriousness of the sexual exploitation or abuse.

### iii. Consolidation of the transportation guidelines

In order to simplify the guidelines, the Commission consolidated §§2G1.1 and 2G1.2 -- the guidelines covering transportation for the purpose of prostitution or other prohibited sexual conduct. Previously, separate guidelines covered the transportation of minors and the transportation of adults. By adding to the consolidated guideline an adjustment that enhances sentences if minors are transported, offenders transporting children are sentenced the same as they would be if the guidelines had been kept separate. In addition, the scope of the consolidated guideline was expanded to cover the new offense created by section 508 of the Telecommunications Act of 1996.

### 2. Recommendation for increased statutory maximum penalties

Under 18 U.S.C. §§ 2251(d) and 2252(b)(1), the maximum term of imprisonment for production, trafficking, and receipt offenses is 10 years. If the offender has a previous federal conviction for a child pornography or sexual abuse crime, a five-year statutory minimum and 15-year, or 180-month, statutory maximum applies. Under 18 U.S.C. §§ 2252(b)(2), the maximum term of imprisonment for possession offenses is five years and no higher statutory maximum is authorized for repeat offenders.

The Commission recommends two changes to the statutory penalties for child pornography offenses. First, Congress should raise the statutory maximum penalties for child pornography production offenses under 18 U.S.C. § 2251 from ten years to fifteen years. Defendants sentenced under §2G2.1 are already subject to high offense levels that result in sentences approaching the statutory maximum, particularly when specific offense characteristics (such as production involving a minor under 12 years of age) apply to enhance the sentence. There also is an increased likelihood that the current statutory maximum would trump sentences under §2G2.1 if the Commission adds other specific offense characteristics to that guideline, such as the five-level pattern of activity enhancement found in §2G2.2 and the two-level computer enhancement adopted by the Commission for §2G2.1 this year. Increasing the statutory maximum for offenses under 18 U.S.C. § 2251 also provides more flexibility for the courts to depart upward from the guideline in particularly egregious cases and makes production a more serious offense than trafficking or receipt. This approach was supported by the Department of Justice in its public comment on the amendments to §2G2.1 that were proposed by the Commission this year.

Second, the Commission recommends that Congress adopt a more uniform approach toward repeat sexual offenders, modeled after 18 U.S.C. § 2247(d). Under the current guidelines and the amendments submitted to Congress in 1996, some repeat offenders will receive guideline ranges that extend above the currently authorized statutory maximum penalties. For example, an offender convicted of production of pornography involving minors under the age of 12 will receive an offense level of 31 (BOL 27 + 4 level adjustment for victim age). If the offender's criminal history score places him in category IV, V or VI, the top of the recommended guideline range would be 188, 210, or 235 months, respectively -- well above the 180-month authorized statutory maximum.

In addition, the approach in 18 U.S.C. § 2247 appears superior to §§ 2251(d) and 2252(b)(1) since it allows both prior federal and state offenses of like kind to trigger the higher statutory maximum. Currently, the higher maximum penalty applies only to pornography offenders with prior federal convictions for sex crimes. In contrast, 18 U.S.C. § 2247 provides for up to a doubling of the statutory maximum for persons with prior federal *or state* sexual abuse crimes. Permitting prior state convictions to count toward increasing the statutory maximum appears justified in order to permit lengthier incarceration of offenders who have shown an increased risk of recidivism, regardless of the forum in which those previous offenses were prosecuted.

The § 2247 approach also avoids imposing mandatory minimum penalties, such as are found in §§ 2251(d) and 2252(b)(1). Such mandatory minimums hinder proportionate sentencing tailored to the individual circumstances of a case, the kind of circumstances that the guidelines take into account. They also prevent judges from departing from mandated minimums in unusual cases that present circumstances not anticipated or inadequately considered by the Commission or by Congress.[48]

### 3. Amendments currently under consideration by the Commission

After undertaking the analysis required by the SCACPA, the Commission is evaluating whether additional modifications to the guidelines covering sex offenses against children may be necessary. The particular options pursued will depend on several factors, including congressional action on pending legislation that may affect the operation of the guidelines in this area, and on the results of public hearings and comments received on the proposals put forward in the next amendment cycle. Options under consideration are described below.

---

[48] For a full discussion of problems created by such legislation, see U.S. SENTENCING COMMISSION, SPECIAL REPORT TO CONGRESS: MANDATORY MINIMUM PENALTIES (1991).

### a. Expand the "pattern of activity" adjustment to possession and production of pornography cases and to the sexual abuse of a minor guideline

One option is to make applicable to §§2G2.1 (production) and 2G2.4 (possession) the five-level enhancement currently contained in the trafficking/receipt guideline 2G2.2(b)(4) "if the defendant engaged in a pattern of activity involving the sexual abuse or exploitation of a minor." The incidence of sexual abuse or exploitation of a minor is prevalent in child pornography production and possession cases as well as child pornography distribution and receipt cases. In addition, the application note that suggests an upward departure in cases that involve actual abuse or exploitation of minors that is not adequately accounted for by the pattern adjustment should be made more generally applicable throughout the pornography guidelines. Application of the enhancement or the upward departure helps ensure lengthier incarceration for offenders convicted of pornography offenses who have engaged in actual abuse of a minor and not only trafficking or possession of pornography depicting such abuse.

In addition, the Commission is exploring three options for increasing punishment for offenders convicted of sexual abuse of a minor. Sentencing under the sexual abuse guidelines is complicated by several factors, however. First, as discussed in the report, the guideline range for aggravated sexual abuse under §2A3.1 is perceived as too high for a significant portion of cases. Conversely, when such cases are sentenced under the sexual abuse of a minor guideline, 2A3.2, the offense level is perceived as too low. The key is to bridge this gap without encouraging undercharging. Second, under current guidelines, if a defendant was not previously convicted of sexual abuse, the punishment does not adequately reflect ongoing or repetitive abusive conduct. Third, many sexual abuse cases involve intra-familial abuse, evidentiary difficulties, and other complicating factors that are not easily taken into account through the application of hard and fast rules. Flexibility and deference to the sentencing judge's superior feel for a case appears warranted.

To address and balance these concerns, the Commission is exploring several different ways to expand the "pattern of activity" adjustment to the sexual abuse guidelines. The Commission could provide for a five-level adjustment in §2A3.2. This would ensure substantially increased punishment for repetitive acts. Case analysis suggests that this adjustment, as modified by the 1996 amendments to §2G2.2, would apply in a substantial majority of sexual abuse cases. Alternatively, the same "pattern of activity" standard might be used as a basis for upward departure rather than as a mandatory five-level adjustment. Such a departure would allow the court to consider any acts of sexual abuse committed by the defendant, whether or not the abuse resulted in conviction, involved more than one victim, or occurred as part of the offense of conviction. The Commission may also consider increasing the base offense level of this guideline.

### b. Clarify the definition of "distribution" of pornography

Currently, §2G2.2 provides for at least a five-level enhancement if the offense involved distribution. Application Note 1 to §2G2.2 states that distribution "includes any act related to distribution for pecuniary gain, including production, transportation, and possession with intent to distribute." It is unclear whether Application Note 1 was intended to limit the enhancement to distribution for pecuniary gain, and the Department of Justice reports that the application note is sometimes read as being inapplicable to non-pecuniary distribution. The definition could be amended to clarify that both distribution for money and other distribution, for example, as part of a barter or trading network, should receive the five-level enhancement.

### c. Consolidate the trafficking/receipt and possession guidelines

As described in the report at Section B.4, defendants convicted of receiving child pornography receive higher sentences than defendants charged with possession, even if they engage in substantially similar conduct. The Commission is considering an amendment to consolidate the trafficking/receipt guideline (§2G2.2) and the possession guideline (§2G2.4). The current trafficking/receipt guideline has a base offense level of 15, and the current possession guideline has a base offense level of 13, both of which will be increased by two levels effective November 1, 1996, subject to congressional disapproval. Consolidation could be accomplished by collapsing the possession and trafficking/receipt guidelines into one guideline. The consolidated guideline would have the higher base offense level of the pre-consolidation trafficking/receipt guideline, but a two-level downward adjustment would apply if the case involved the receipt or possession of fewer than 10 items with no intended distribution. Under this approach, sentences for certain receipt cases would be two levels lower than they would be under the amended guidelines submitted to Congress this year.

In 1991, the Commission reported similar concerns about the disparity between receipt and possession sentences and it amended the guidelines so that receipt cases were sentenced under the possession guideline. But this amendment was overridden by Congress through enactment of Section 632 of Public Law 102-141, the Treasury, Postal Service and General Government Appropriations Act of 1992. The Commission was directed to increase base offense levels for trafficking and receipt (§2G2.2) (from level 13 to level 15) and for possession (§2G2.4) (from level 10 to level 13). The instruction also provided that §2G2.4 shall apply only to offense conduct involving simple possession. Offenses involving receipt and trafficking were to be sentenced under the new higher offense levels prescribed by §2G2.2. The Commission promulgated the mandated amendments, which took effect November 27, 1991. Because Congress has previously directed the Commission to sentence receipt cases under the trafficking guideline rather than the possession guideline, additional legislation may be needed for the Commission to make the changes being considered here.

Despite this statutory history, several factors lead the Commission to conclude that the present approach to the sentencing of receipt and possession cases should be reevaluated. First, there still appears to be disparity in the sentencing of substantially similar crimes, and there is some indication that judges may be trying to avoid such disparity. Second, in response to the Congressional directive in SCACPA, the Commission has already proposed a two-level increase in the base offense level for all trafficking, receipt and possession cases (proposed to be effective November 1, 1996 subject to Congressional disapproval). Thus, even though the consolidation being considered would decrease offense levels (and therefore sentences) in some receipt cases by two levels, offense levels would not drop below where they are now pending the increase proposed to take effect in November. In effect, the consolidation would nullify the two-level increase proposed to take effect November 1, 1996, and keep certain receipt sentences at their current level while allowing trafficking and possession sentences to increase. Third, the consolidation approach recommended here will actually increase the punishment for some possession cases by making the specific offense characteristics, now available for receipt, available for possession as well. In particular, the specific offense characteristics of §2G2.2 would also apply to possession cases. These include a two-level enhancement for sadistic or masochistic material and the five-level adjustment if the defendant engaged in a pattern of activity of sexual abuse or exploitation.